STEM
IN OUR WORLD

SPORTS TECHNOLOGY:
Cryotherapy, LED Courts, and More

BY JOHN WOOD
& IMOGEN RAMSDALE

STEM
IN OUR WORLD

THE SECRET BOOK COMPANY

©2019
The Secret Book Company
King's Lynn
Norfolk PE30 4LS

ISBN: 978-1-78998-035-6

All rights reserved
Printed in Malaysia

Written by:
John Wood & Imogen Ramsdale

Edited by:
Holly Duhig

Designed by:
Daniel Scase

A catalogue record for this book
is available from the British Library.

CONTENTS

WORDS THAT LOOK LIKE **THIS** ARE EXPLAINED IN THE GLOSSARY ON PAGE 31.

WELCOME TO STEM SCHOOL

MEET YOUR TEACHER

Attention, students. My name is Professor Tess Tube, and I am your teacher. Oh, this? This is a deadly laser gun that I'm looking after for a friend. I thought I'd bring it along to class just in case one of you misbehaves... No, wait! Don't run away! I'm only joking! I would never waste lasers on you lot. No, you are here for a completely different reason – by reading this book, you are now part of STEM School. STEM stands for:

SCIENCE, TECHNOLOGY, ENGINEERING AND MATHS

But STEM isn't all about deadly laser guns. STEM is important in all sorts of ways.

Why Is STEM Important in All Sorts of Ways?

You can probably find STEM in almost every part of your life. Here are a few examples:

- Computers at school, which help us learn
- Toasters, kettles and ovens at home, which help us make food and drink
- Hospital machines and medicine, which help us live longer
- Cars, boats and planes, which help us travel around the world quickly
- Weather reports, which tell us what the weather is going to be like

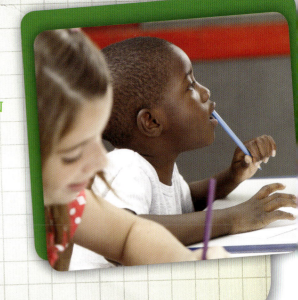

STEM is all about understanding and solving problems in the real world. When we have an idea of how something might work, we test it again and again to make sure it is right. Then we can create machines and **SYSTEMS** to solve the problems we have.

Sometimes we get new information about how things work, and find out that our old ideas were wrong. But that is OK – STEM subjects are all about changing your ideas based on the information you have.

REMEMBER, CHILDREN, THIS WON'T BE EASY. WE'D BETTER LIMBER UP FIRST AND DO SOME SCIENCE WARM-UPS. THAT'S RIGHT; LET'S STRETCH THOSE BRAINS. MAYBE POWERLIFT SOME CLIPBOARDS. OR RUN ROUND A MICROSCOPE. ARE YOU READY TO START? GOOD, BECAUSE WE'VE GOT SCIENCE TO DO! LET'S SEE WHAT WE ARE LEARNING ABOUT TODAY...

STEM AND SPORTS

HOW MANY SPORTS ARE THERE?

There are many sports that exist today, but the exact number depends on what you think a sport is. Do you think cycling is a sport? What about horse riding? Both are part of the **OLYMPICS**. Whatever the **DEFINITION** of a sport actually is, most people agree that there are hundreds of them! People have been playing sports throughout history. You might even recognise some of them.

THE WORLD SPORTS ENCYCLOPAEDIA SAYS THAT THERE ARE OVER 8,000 SPORTS. AROUND 30 ARE CURRENTLY AT THE OLYMPICS.

FAMOUS SPORTS THROUGHOUT HISTORY

The first Olympic Games were held in Olympia, Greece, over 2,700 years ago in 776 BC. The only sport was a short **SPRINT**, or race. The ancient Aztecs played a sport called Tlachtli. The players would hit a ball with their hips, and try and get it through a hoop. Sports such as this were very popular among the Aztecs and other civilisations in ancient America.

A DRAWING OF CUJU

THE RUINS OF OLYMPIA

Cuju was a game played by ancient Chinese civilisations from at least AD 55. It was a game in which people kicked balls into nets, so it may have been a little bit like today's football.

Sports are very different today. There are all sorts of technology and improvements that make it safer and more exciting.

Also, **ATHLETES** and players can now train harder and better than before, which makes them faster and stronger.

GAMES SUCH AS FOOTBALL CAN ONLY BE WON IF YOU WORK TOGETHER AS A TEAM.

Not only is sport fun to watch and play, but it also keeps us fit and healthy. Playing sports can help you get better at teamwork, and help you make new friends. Sport is an important part of our lives, and so there is lots of STEM research to do.

BRRRRRRRIIIII NNNNNGGGGG!

AH, THE BELL! IT LOOKS LIKE THE LESSONS ARE ABOUT TO BEGIN. ROLL UP YOUR SLEEVES, STUDENTS, WE ARE GOING TO TAKE A LOOK AT STEM IN ACTION. LET'S TURN THE PAGE AND SEE WHAT WE'RE GOING TO LEARN ABOUT FIRST...

INSTANT REPLAY TECHNOLOGY

A SECOND PAIR OF EYES

REFEREES can't see everything. This can be a problem, especially if everybody is arguing about whether a football crossed the goal line, or if a tennis ball was in or out. Referees are needed because they can make fair decisions but, if they didn't see what happened, they might have to guess. This can completely ruin a game!

Technology has been invented which uses computers and mathematics to help referees know exactly what happened. This makes the game fairer for all players.

REFEREE

HAWK-EYE

Hawk-Eye is a type of technology that is used in lots of sports, such as football, cricket and tennis. It uses around ten different cameras to tell where the ball landed or where it was going.

Hawk-Eye then uses this information to work out what probably happened, and creates a **VIRTUAL** video. The referee can watch the video and make a decision.

IN TENNIS, HAWK-EYE SHOWS A VIRTUAL VIDEO WHICH SHOWS WHETHER THE BALL WAS IN OR OUT.

8.54   ROLEX

ROLEX IN

STATISTICS

Even the best cameras in the world can't see exactly what happens all the time. To be as accurate as possible, Hawk-Eye uses statistics.

Statistics is a type of mathematics which uses information, or data, to draw **CONCLUSIONS** about what happened.

LET'S DO SOME STATISTICS!

TESS'S LAB →

IF WE COUNTED THE NUMBER OF EXPLOSIONS THAT HAPPEN IN MY SCIENCE LAB FOR A DAY, WE MIGHT FIND THAT THERE ARE 11 EXPLOSIONS. THE NEXT DAY THERE MIGHT BE 13 EXPLOSIONS, AND ANOTHER 12 EXPLOSIONS THE DAY AFTER THAT! NOW WE HAVE A MUCH BETTER IDEA OF HOW MANY EXPLOSIONS TEND TO HAPPEN IN MY LABORATORY EVERY DAY – IT WILL PROBABLY BE AROUND 12. THE INFORMATION WE'VE COLLECTED ABOUT THE NUMBER OF EXPLOSIONS IS CALLED OUR DATA.

THE MORE DATA YOU COLLECT OVER TIME, THE BETTER YOUR CONCLUSIONS WILL BE.

HAWK-EYE THE MATHEMATICIAN

Hawk-Eye has a lot of data which tells it how far balls travel when they are hit. Hawk-Eye compares the speed and direction of the real ball to its data, then works out where the ball probably landed. Hawk-Eye is so accurate because the cameras look very carefully, and the computer uses lots and lots of data.

HAWK-EYE USES CAMERAS WHICH ARE POSITIONED AROUND THE FIELD.

9

LED COURTS

School gyms and playgrounds often have lots of different lines and markings painted on the floor. These lines make it easier to play different sports and games. However, there is a new type of sports gym which looks a little different. With new **LED** court technology, the lines will be made with lights inside a glass floor. The lights could make any pattern or shape imaginable, so any sport could be played. The floor could also show scores or any other information about the game.

Some LED courts are also **INTERACTIVE**, such as the House of Mamba basketball court. This LED technology can tell where the player is on the court. It can also set out **VISUAL** training programs to follow by showing the players where to put their feet, or where they need to run to next. This shows the players where they are making mistakes, and helps them train in a fun and interactive way.

I NEED TO GET ONE OF THESE INTERACTIVE LED COURTS. SOME OF THESE SPORTS ARE MORE CONFUSING THAN THE MYSTERIES OF THE UNIVERSE!

LED Lights

At the moment, interactive courts are very expensive. The House of Mamba court is kept in a special building. The floor uses LED lights because they are tough and use very little electricity. LED lights do not heat up like old-fashioned light bulbs, which makes them much safer too. The lights in an interactive LED court, such as the House of Mamba, are controlled using a computer. When a lot of LEDs are lined up in a grid, they can create all sorts of pictures and patterns.

LED LIGHTS COME IN ALL SHAPES AND SIZES.

Unbreakable Glass

Even though people play rough sports on the LED glass floor, nothing gets damaged. The floor is made from a special type of very tough glass. The glass is specially *TREATED* so it isn't slippery.

LED courts are made so that balls can bounce and people can run in the same way they would on a normal court.

11

SENSOR TECHNOLOGY

CONNECTED TECHNOLOGY

Sensors are pieces of technology that can sense the world around them. An automatic door has a sensor which tells the door to open if it senses movement. Some sports equipment uses sensors, or 'connected sensor technology', to sense what the player is doing. This is called 'connected sports equipment'.

STREET LIGHTS HAVE LIGHT SENSORS THAT TELL THE LAMPS TO TURN ON WHEN IT GETS DARK.

SMART BAT AND CONNECTED TENNIS RACKETS

Smart Bat is a piece of connected sensor technology for baseball players. The sensor fits inside the handle of the baseball bat and tracks the angle and speed of the swing. This information is then sent to an app, which gives the player tips on how to improve their swing.

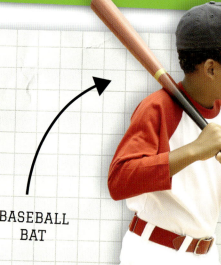

BASEBALL BAT

There is also a connected tennis racket with similar technology. It has motion sensors inside the handle that track the speed and angle of the swing. It also has pressure sensors on the strings that can sense which area of the racket hits the ball.

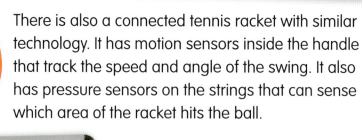

HERE WE GO, THE SENSOR IS ABOUT TO TELL ME HOW TO IMPROVE. IT SAYS... HOLD THE RACKET THE RIGHT WAY ROUND. OH, I SEE. WHOOPS.

TENNIS RACKET

Smart Clothing

'Smart clothing technology' is clothing that can sense how fast your heart beats, or how quickly you breathe. It can also be worn at night to record what position you sleep in.

Smart clothing technology might also measure biosignals. Biosignals are signals sent from the brain to the muscles. The clothing uses **ELECTRODES** to turn biosignals into electrical signals. These electrical signals are sent to a device, which warns the athlete if they are training too hard.

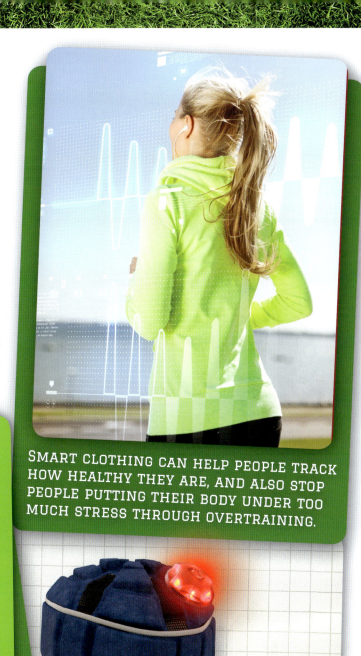

SMART CLOTHING CAN HELP PEOPLE TRACK HOW HEALTHY THEY ARE, AND ALSO STOP PEOPLE PUTTING THEIR BODY UNDER TOO MUCH STRESS THROUGH OVERTRAINING.

HUMANS HAVE AROUND 80 BILLION BRAIN CELLS, SOME OF WHICH ARE FIRING SIGNALS ALL THE TIME. THAT'S A LOT OF BRAIN SIGNALS!

Sensors for Safety

In contact sports such as rugby or American football, players jump on other players and tackle them to the ground. Sports such as these can be dangerous when played by strong professionals. If a player receives a serious bump to the head, they might get a brain injury called a concussion. Players might not realise they have a concussion straight away. To stop this, sensors can be placed inside hats or helmets. The sensors glow red if there is a strong bump to the head. The player is then checked for signs of concussion.

PLAYERS MIGHT NOT REALISE THEY HAVE A CONCUSSION STRAIGHT AWAY. IF THE CONCUSSION IS SERIOUS AND THEY DO NOT SEE A DOCTOR, THIS CAN BE DANGEROUS.

SUPER MATERIALS

Technology is also improving the material that sports equipment is made from. Carbon fibre is often used for sports equipment because it is extremely strong and light.

What Is Carbon Fibre?

Carbon fibre is a mixture of two materials. For golf clubs and other similar sports equipment, the first material is usually something hard and **RIGID** such as plastic. The plastic is joined with a special kind of carbon.

EXPENSIVE GOLF CLUBS MIGHT BE MADE OUT OF CARBON FIBRE.

This is how this special kind of carbon is made:

- FIRST, A MATERIAL WHICH HAS CARBON IN IT IS STRETCHED OUT AND HEATED TO A VERY HIGH TEMPERATURE, UNTIL EVERYTHING IS HEATED AWAY APART FROM THE CARBON.

- THE LEFTOVER CARBON IS TIGHTLY LINKED TOGETHER IN LONG, STRONG, LADDER-LIKE SHAPES, CALLED FIBRES.

- THESE FIBRES ARE THEN JOINED WITH THE PLASTIC TO CREATE A SUPER-STRONG, CARBON FIBRE PLASTIC.

OKAY, THIS CARBON FIBRE IS A LOT TOUGHER THAN I THOUGHT.

SHEET OF CARBON FIBRE

Carbon Fibre Vaulting Poles

Materials such as carbon fibre are very important in pole vaulting. Pole vaulting is an Olympic event where the athlete runs towards a high bar while carrying a big pole. As they get near to the bar, they stick the pole in the ground, causing it to bend. As the pole straightens, the athlete uses it to help them jump over the high bar. However, the sport was played very differently in the past. Athletes used to use wooden or bamboo poles, which didn't bend very much at all. It was much harder to use these poles, so people were not able to jump as high.

THE WORLD RECORD FOR POLE VAULTING WAS SET IN THE 1990s. NOBODY HAS BEEN ABLE TO BEAT IT SINCE, PARTLY BECAUSE CARBON FIBRE TECHNOLOGY HAS NOT CHANGED OR IMPROVED VERY MUCH.

THE WORLD RECORD FOR POLE VAULTING IS 6.14 METRES HIGH. THAT'S TALLER THAN A GIRAFFE!

Fibreglass

Today, some vaulting poles are made of fibreglass. Fibreglass is used because it is strong, light and very bendable. Fibreglass is made by melting glass and then squeezing it through tubes to form long, extremely thin threads. The threads are woven together and mixed with another material, such as plastic or *RESIN*.

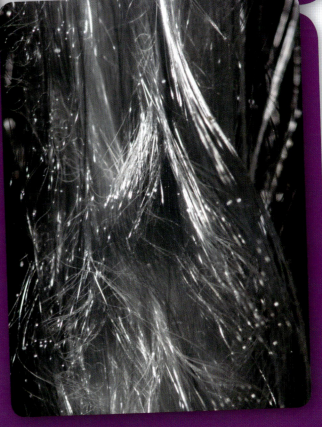

CLOSE-UP IMAGE OF FIBREGLASS THREADS

GENETICS

Everything about a person, from what they like to how they look, is affected by genetics. The science of genetics is all about the *TRAITS* that are *INHERITED* from our parents. Today, genetics is being used to help young athletes get better at sports. Some scientists think that genetics may be able to tell athletes what they should eat, how they should train and what sports they will be good at. But first, a quick lesson on how genetics works.

GENETICS DECIDES WHAT FEATURES YOU INHERIT FROM YOUR PARENTS, SUCH AS YOUR EYE COLOUR, HAIR COLOUR OR THE SHAPE OF YOUR NOSE.

CELLS AND DNA

Our bodies are made up of trillions of cells. Every single cell has a set of *DNA*, which is a list of instructions about how to make a living thing. When cells are growing and maintaining the body, they check the DNA to make sure they are making it in the right way. The instructions that the DNA carries is called the genetic code. The genetic code decides things such as how tall a person is or the colour of their hair.

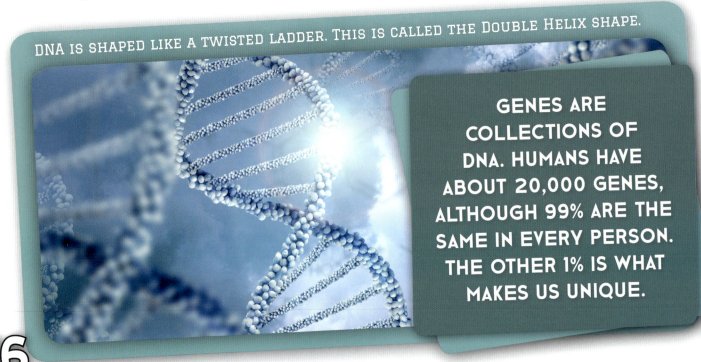

DNA IS SHAPED LIKE A TWISTED LADDER. THIS IS CALLED THE DOUBLE HELIX SHAPE.

GENES ARE COLLECTIONS OF DNA. HUMANS HAVE ABOUT 20,000 GENES, ALTHOUGH 99% ARE THE SAME IN EVERY PERSON. THE OTHER 1% IS WHAT MAKES US UNIQUE.

THE FOOD GENES

By looking at the genetic code, it may be possible to tell exactly what kind of food and diet is needed to help the body the most. For example, some people might have trouble digesting or absorbing certain **NUTRIENTS**. They might need to take a **DIETARY SUPPLEMENT** to stay healthy. This kind of information is stored in certain genes, which decide how the body digests food and nutrients.

SPORTS PEOPLE FOLLOW HEALTHY DIETS ANYWAY, BUT THEIR GENETIC CODE MIGHT TELL THEM HOW TO EAT AN EVEN BETTER DIET.

RUNNING IN THE FAMILY

Some companies will look at someone's genetic code and tell them what sort of training suits them the most. To look at someone's genetic code, the company might use a special cotton swab to collect saliva from inside the mouth. The saliva contains cells, which have DNA inside. Once scientists have looked at the DNA, they can tell what sort of sport a person might be naturally good at. For example, some people might find it easier to run faster or farther than other people.

DNA COTTON SWAB AND TEST TUBE

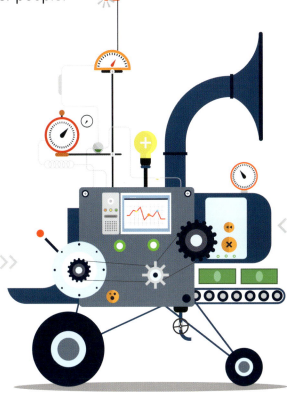

OOH, I'M ABOUT TO FIND OUT MY RESULT!

THE SPORT YOU WOULD BE BEST AT IS... EGG-THROWING.

WHAT? THAT'S NOT A SPORT!

YES IT IS. GO LONG.

17

HORMONES

What Are Hormones?

Hormones are **CHEMICAL** messages that tell the body to do things. There are lots of different types of hormones that are sent between different parts of the body, and they all do different things. For example, there is a hormone called ghrelin, which is released by the stomach. Ghrelin is used to tell the brain and the rest of the body that the stomach is empty. When exercising, a chemical called serotonin is released. Serotonin makes people feel happy.

THESE ARE GLANDS, WHICH ARE PARTS OF THE BODY THAT CREATE HORMONES. THESE GLANDS CREATE ADRENALINE, WHICH IS A HORMONE THAT MAKES YOUR HEART BEAT FASTER.

ARE YOU... SURE EXERCISE RELEASES *WHEEZE* SEROTONIN? BECAUSE I REALLY DON'T FEEL TOO... *GASP* HAPPY RIGHT NOW. I MAINLY FEEL SWEATY.

Other Useful Hormones

Serotonin isn't the only thing released while exercising. Human growth hormone, or HGH for short, is also made by the body during exercise. This hormone helps the body grow more cells to build bigger muscles. This is useful for people who want to get stronger or faster. The more a person exercises, the more HGH is released.

EXTRA HORMONES

Scientists are able to create hormones **ARTIFICIALLY**. A hormone can be created by mixing the right chemicals together. Artificial hormones are often used in medicine to help people grow, or feel happier. However, some artificial hormones are not allowed in sport.

HORMONES ARE PUT IN THE BODY USING AN INJECTION OR A PILL.

DOPING

When athletes use drugs or hormones that will help them win, it is called doping. Doping is not allowed because it gives the athlete an unfair **ADVANTAGE**. A hormone such as HGH might be taken in order to build more muscle. A hormone such as erythropoietin, or EPO for short, might be taken because it makes the body create more red blood cells. More red blood cells means more oxygen is sent to the muscles to help them work faster.

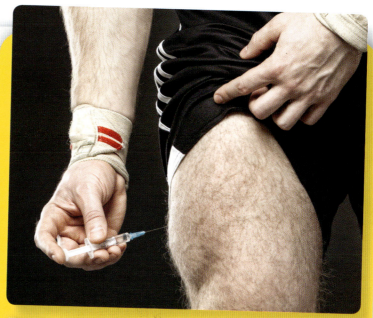

EXTRA HORMONES CAN BE DANGEROUS TO THE BODY.

BIONIC BODIES

PROSTHETICS

Limbs (your arms and legs) are very important. We use them every day to use things and move around. There are many people who do not have four limbs. These people might use prosthetics instead. A prosthetic is a human-made replacement for a body part, and is made out of non-living materials. Prosthetic limbs help people do everyday things, such as running or holding things.

PROSTHETIC ARM

WAIT, RUNNING IS AN EVERYDAY THING? THAT'S THE WEIRDEST THING I'VE LEARNED TODAY.

RUNNING BLADES

If a person doesn't have two legs, it doesn't stop them from doing well in sports. There are many special prosthetic limbs made for use in sport, such as running blades. These blades are curved, and are made from carbon fibre. The blades are also bendy, which helps the athlete run faster.

RUNNING BLADES

IN 2012, AN ATHLETE USING RUNNING BLADES WAS ALLOWED TO COMPETE AGAINST NON-DISABLED ATHLETES IN THE OLYMPICS FOR THE FIRST TIME. HE CAME IN SECOND PLACE.

Bionic Limbs

In the future, prosthetic limbs may be replaced by bionic limbs. Bionic limbs are currently being tested all over the world. Bionic limbs are special because they are controlled by the person's brain, just like a **BIOLOGICAL** limb.

A BRAIN-CONTROLLED BIONIC ARM

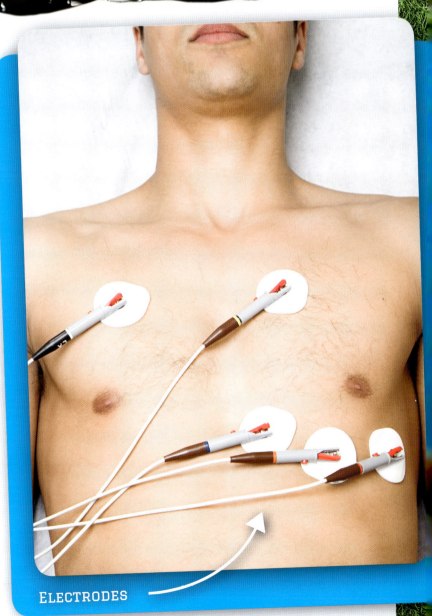

How Do Bionic Limbs Work?

If a person has lost a limb, there will still be **NERVES** connecting the brain to the area where the limb was lost. If these nerves aren't too damaged, they can be rewired to different muscles, usually in the chest. This means that any brain signal sent to the arm goes to the chest instead. Brain signals are just electrical signals. Electrical signals can be picked up by electrodes, which are placed on the chest. The electrodes are then connected to the bionic limb. Now, when the brain sends a signal to the arm, it actually goes to the electrodes on the chest which tell the bionic limb to move. The person can then move their bionic limb using their brain.

ELECTRODES

SWIMSUIT TO SPACESUIT

BREAKING WORLD RECORDS

In 2009, the World Aquatics Championship was held in Italy. Swimmers came from all over the world to find out who was the fastest. However, something strange happened: 43 swimming records were broken, which is a lot. The reason for this was a new technology in the swimsuits. Because the suits helped the athletes swim amazingly fast, some people called it 'technology-doping'. Even though the athletes who used these suits were very talented, many people worried that the sport should be about the swimming, instead of the technology. The suits are now banned.

98% OF THE MEDALS WON IN THE 2009 CHAMPIONSHIP WERE WON BY PEOPLE WEARING THE NEW SUITS.

A SECOND SKIN

The banned swimsuits covered much of the swimmer's body and stuck very close to the skin. The snug swimsuit helped swimmers travel through the water smoother and faster. Normal swimsuits have bits of clothing which stick out and catch more water, which slows the swimmer down. This is called drag. A smooth swimsuit stopped this happening, and helped the swimmer glide easily through the water.

A *STREAMLINED* SWIMMER WILL HAVE LESS DRAG SLOWING THEM DOWN.

GETTING RID OF DRAG

The suits were also covered with panels of polyurethane, or PU for short. PU is a material that is like a cross between rubber and plastic. Unlike the swimsuits that swimmers used to wear, PU suits were very good at gliding through water without being slowed down.

A BANNED SWIMSUIT

Similar technology to the swimsuits has been used in other parts of the world. Astronauts and scientists who want to explore space are developing something called a biosuit. Unlike a normal, bulky spacesuit, the biosuits are made to snugly fit the astronaut's body like a second skin. The advantage of the tight biosuit is that it helps the astronauts move around more freely when they are in space.

THE BIOSUIT, WHICH IS ON THE LEFT, WILL ALSO HAVE SENSORS AND OTHER TECHNOLOGY INSIDE.

I'D LOVE TO BE A SWIMMER, BUT MY LAB COAT CREATES TOO MUCH DRAG. WHAT DO YOU MEAN 'DON'T WEAR THE LAB COAT'? ARE YOU MAD? WHAT IF THERE IS SOME EMERGENCY SCIENCE THAT NEEDS TO BE DONE? NO, IT IS FAR TOO RISKY. I'D BETTER KEEP THE COAT ON.

FORCE PLATFORMS

RUNNING FORCES

A force is an invisible flow of energy. Many forces push or pull things. When we walk or run, we create a force by pushing our feet against the ground. The ground creates an equal force back to us, and this is what pushes us forward when we run. A force platform is a piece of technology that measures how much force a person makes as they push against the ground. Force platforms are useful in sport because the amount of force an athlete *EXERTS* can say a lot about how they run or how well-balanced they are.

FORCE PLATES

HOW DO FORCE PLATFORMS WORK?

A simple force platform is made up of two metal plates with sensors sandwiched between them. There are usually four sensors, one in each corner of the plates. When something pushes on the sensors, they detect this force and release an electric signal. The more the sensors are pushed, the stronger the electric signal is. The signal is sent to a computer, which records the strength of the force.

> **FORCE PLATFORM SENSORS WILL GIVE OFF STRONGER OR WEAKER ELECTRIC SIGNALS, DEPENDING ON WHICH PART IS STEPPED ON.**

SENSING THE FORCE

Force platforms are used in all sorts of sports, but they are most useful when measuring running. This can be done by having the athlete run over the force platform, or by using sensors that are placed inside a shoe. This means the bottom of the shoe can measure the force.

USING THE FORCE

One of the main uses of a force platform is to prevent injuries. Force platforms can be used alongside other information to work out if a person is running in an incorrect way, which will give them an injury later on. For example, if a person runs in a way that puts too much strain on one area of the foot, it might cause damage to that area after lots of running.

ALL THIS RUNNING ABOUT HAS GIVEN ME AN INJURY. I GUESS THAT MEANS I DON'T HAVE TO PLAY ANY MORE SPORTS TODAY! OH WAIT, APPARENTLY THERE IS A TREATMENT FOR INJURIES ON THE NEXT PAGE. SOMETHING CALLED 'CRYOTHERAPY'.
RATS. I MEAN... YAY.

CRYOTHERAPY

THE TECHNOLOGY OF FROZEN PEAS

Cryotherapy is a way of treating injuries with cold temperatures. While the technology used in cryotherapy is complicated, it is based on a simple idea that cold temperatures can help some injuries. We do this all the time when we put a bag of ice or frozen peas on a bump or a sprain. The cold temperature makes the blood vessels narrow, meaning less fluid can reach the injured area to cause a *SWELLING*. The cold temperature also slows your nerves cells down, which lessens the pain because fewer pain signals are sent to the brain.

SPORTS DOCTORS NEVER PUT A BAG OF ICE DIRECTLY ON THE SKIN FOR A LONG TIME. THIS CAN CAUSE *FROSTBITE*. INSTEAD, THE BAG OF ICE IS PLACED OVER THE CLOTHES OF THE INJURED AREA.

CRYOTHERAPY IN SPORT

Sports use all sorts of technology for cryotherapy, and it is usually a little more complicated than a bag of frozen peas. Cold gel packs that are colder than ice are often used. Sometimes a freeze spray, called a *VAPOUR*-coolant, is used. Inside the vapour-coolant is a cooling gas, or vapour, which is sprayed on the injury when a trigger is pulled.

GEL PACK

VAPOUR-COOLANT

CRYOCHAMBERS

Another type of cryotherapy takes place in something called a cryochamber. This is like a small and extremely cold room or machine which athletes sit in. **NITROGEN** gas is used to freeze the air inside the chamber. The temperatures can be as low as -160 degrees Celsius (°C). To help imagine how cold that is, remember that water freezes solid at 0°C. Because the temperatures are so low, players only stay in the cryochamber for a few minutes. Thick woollen socks and mittens are also worn to protect fingers and toes from frostbite.

SPORTS TEAMS SAY THAT CRYOCHAMBERS HELP PLAYERS RECOVER FROM TRAINING AND INJURIES FASTER.

LACK OF TESTING

However, although some forms of cryotherapy, such as ice packs, are known to help, cryochambers have not had the same amount of scientific testing. It is not clear how useful the chamber is, so more testing needs to be done.

BRRR... BEING A SPORTS PERSON IS N-NOT EASY. ONE M-MINUTE YOU ARE HOT AND SWEATY, AND THE NEXT MINUTE YOU ARE F-F-FREEZING COLD! NOT TO MENTION HOW HARD ALL THESE S-SPORTS ARE! I CAN'T DO ANY OF THEM. YOU KNOW, I TH-THINK I'LL JUST BE THE REFEREE.

27

THE FUTURE OF STEM IN SPORTS

DO YOU THINK YOU KNOW WHAT IS GOING TO HAPPEN IN THE FUTURE? WELL, WHATEVER HAPPENS, WE ARE GOING TO NEED LOTS OF BRIGHT NEW SCIENTISTS, ENGINEERS AND MATHEMATICIANS. HERE ARE SOME OF THE THINGS THAT THEY MIGHT BE WORKING ON...

ESPORTS

Esports are a new type of sport involving video games. They are the fastest-growing sports in the world. Lots of people come to watch in huge stadiums, and many more watch online. All sorts of video games are played, including football games, real-time *STRATEGY* games and first-person shooter games. Although they are not like traditional sports, esports are played in many places all over the world, and we could see esports being played in the Olympics one day.

Although they are not physical like traditional sports, esports use lots of sporty skills, such as quick reaction times, thinking hard about strategies and working together as a team. Esports may be included in even more sporting competitions in the future.

ESPORTS

VIRTUAL REALITY

Virtual reality is a type of technology which can simulate anything. By using headsets, headphones and other devices, people can feel as if they are really in a computer program. Today, people can use virtual reality to simulate a sports game so they can practise strategies. In the future of sport, virtual reality may become a popular way for players to train. Virtual reality training would be a good way to practise what to do in a game without needing other people to practise with you. There is also a reduced risk of injury during practice.

VIRTUAL
REALITY
HEADSET

TECHNOLOGY DOPING

However, maybe the world of sports won't change in the way we think. As we have seen throughout this book, there are many examples of technologies that have been banned because they make sports too easy, or give people an unfair advantage. What do you think? Should some technology be banned? Is sport all about the person, or should we embrace technology and see what it can help us do?

HOME TIME

BRRRRRRRI.NNNNNGGGG

THERE'S THE BELL. IT LOOKS LIKE ANOTHER DAY AT STEM SCHOOL HAS COME TO AN END. AND, TO FINISH OFF YOUR SPORTS DAY, YOU'RE GOING TO RUN HOME! ON YOUR MARKS, GET SET, GO!

ZAP

WHOOPS, I THINK I MIXED UP THE LASER GUN AND STARTER PISTOL. I THINK IT'S BEST IF I GIVE THIS BACK TO MY FRIEND NOW. IF YOU LIKE STEM AND WANT TO LEARN MORE, THEN READ ON...

FIND OUT MORE

You could see if your school has any after-school STEM programs. Try talking to your teacher or your parents about how to get involved in STEM. You could also try thinking like a scientist, mathematician or engineer yourself! STEM is all about solving problems – next time you see a problem, think about how it can be solved. You might be able to test your idea and see if it works. That is what STEM is all about.

FOLLOW THESE LINKS TO CARRY ON LEARNING ONLINE:

BBC SCIENCE
– http://www.bbc.co.uk/education/subjects/z6svr82

BBC MATHS
– http://www.bbc.co.uk/education/subjects/zjxhfg8

CRASH COURSE SCIENCE VIDEOS
– www.youtube.com/user/crashcoursekids

GLOSSARY

ADVANTAGE — to be in a better position than someone else

ARTIFICIALLY — in a way that is made by humans

ATHLETES — people who are skilled at sport or other types of physical exercise

BIOLOGICAL — relating to living things

CELLS — the basic units that make up all living things

CHEMICAL — a substance that materials are made from

CONCLUSIONS — judgements and ideas based on information

DEFINITION — the meaning of a word

DIETARY SUPPLEMENT — something that can be ingested that contains extra nutrition

DNA — a type of acid that carries the genetic information in cells

ELECTRODES — electric conductors used to transfer electricity to nonconductive materials

EXERTS — applies or uses

FROSTBITE — injury caused by extremely cold temperatures

INHERITED — passed down from a parent

INTERACTIVE — something that communicates and changes based on interaction

LED — light-emitting diode; an electrical device that gives off light

OLYMPICS — an event held every four years in which athletes compete in various sports

NERVES — the white, string-like fibres that stretch all through the body and send messages to and from the brain

NITROGEN — a type of gas

NUTRIENTS — natural substances that plants and animals need to grow and stay healthy

REFEREES — sports officials that make sure players are following the rules of the game

RESIN — a thick, slimy substance that can become hard

RIGID — stiff and unbendable

SPRINT — a very fast run over a short distance

STRATEGY — a plan of action to win

STREAMLINED — smoothly shaped to travel quicker through gas or liquid

SWELLING — becoming larger and rounder in size

SYSTEMS — sets of things that work together to do specific jobs

TRAITS — qualities or characteristics of a person

TREATED — applied with a substance in order to protect or preserve it

VAPOUR — a substance in the gaseous state

VIRTUAL — something that is simulated by computers, but does not exist in the real world

VISUAL — to do with seeing or the eyes

INDEX

PHOTO CREDITS

Front Cover – mikser45, mikser45, Vereshchagin Dmitry, Mega Pixel alexytrener. 4 – Lorena Fernandez. 5 – wavebreakmedia. 6 – DJTaylor, Izabela Miszczak, wikicommons. 7 – sportpoint, matimix. 8 – LightField Studios, wikicommons. 9 – wikicommons. 10 – PhawKStudio, EFKS, Catsence, Eugene Onischenko. 11 – Sky vectors, DK samco, Mariusz S. Jurgielewicz. 12 – Janthiwa Sutthiboriban, Monkey Business Images, Pavel L Photo and Video. 13 – Syda Productions, Mauro Rodrigues, Pop_Studio. 14 – Patrick Foto, wikicommons. 15 – Racheal Grazias, bonzodog. 16 – LightField Studios, Natali_ Mis. 17 – Antonina Vlasova, IvanRiver, PODIS. 18 – D. Kucharski K. Kucharska, ARTSIOM ZAVADSKI, Denis Kuvaev. 19 – evkaz, luckyraccoon. 20 – Fanfo, mezzotint. 21 – wikicommons, XiXinXing. 22 – pio3, Boris Ryaposov, wikicommons. 23 – wikicommons. 24 – GlebSStock, wikicommons. 25 – Syda Productions, Robert Przybysz. 26 – TinnaPong, Melodia plus photos, Laszlo66. 27 – Maylat, BlurryMe. 28 – Gorodenkoff. 29 – KK Tan, vectorfusionart. 30 – Rawpixel.com. Border on all pages: rangizzz. Graph Paper – The_Pixel. Tess Tube – mayrum. Images are courtesy of Shutterstock.com. With thanks to Getty Images, Thinkstock Photo and iStockphoto.